MW00895822

ME AND MY BODY

CONTENTS

INTRODUCTION	1
MY BODY	4
MY SENSES	12
HEALTHY LIVING	18
THE LIFE CYCLE	26

About this book

Me and my body is packed full of useful resources and practical lessons for children in Key Stage 1/Primary 1–3 classes. The lesson plans will help teachers to cover the curriculum for early understanding about human life and safe, healthy living in a comprehensive way, while giving children opportunities to discover and learn key pieces of knowledge.

This book is divided into four sections: *My body*, *My senses*, *Healthy living* and *The life cycle*. The A1 poster provided with the book offers resources to focus and enrich your work on each of these themes: a picture of people at different ages, to encourage comparison and the use of correct vocabulary; a labelled skeleton, to show 'what's on the inside'; and a diagram of a typical day's activities, to promote discussion about healthy living. The poster is used throughout the lesson plans, which are also backed up with photocopiable resource pages.

INTRODUCTION

About 'Me and my body'

Strategies for teaching about 'Me and my body' with Key Stage 1/Primary 1–3 children should focus on the children's own fundamental knowledge about themselves. You should remember three key questions when planning for this unit of work:

◆ *What can the children do (in terms of their physical activity)?*
◆ *How can they do it?*
◆ *Why does it happen like this?*

Addressing these three questions helps to direct the overall teaching, and the children's learning, towards the key aspects of knowledge required by the curriculum documents. 'Me and my body' is a scientific theme that every child will be able to contribute towards, since the main teaching resource is the child him/herself. Positive use should also be made of knowledge and information collected by parents and carers of the children.

Problems to look out for

When teaching about 'Me and my body', it is important to keep the following points in mind.

◆ Make it clear that the skeleton is not a 'scary thing' distinct from the body: we all have one. It is simply the body's framework.
◆ In talking about food and diets, emphasise that there are no 'bad foods', only bad diets.
◆ Be aware of issues related to race and gender.
◆ Take care in planning to include all the children, regardless of their level of ability or of any disability.
◆ Treat all issues openly and in a sensitive manner.
◆ Take care to distinguish between recreational drugs (which are usually harmful) and medicines (which can help if used correctly).
◆ Some children may be shy and sensitive about discussing the body. If so, do not press them into the discussion; allow them to join in as their confidence develops.
◆ If you are in doubt about anything, consult with parents (either by meeting them or by writing).

Gaining confidence

Children will come to the subject with an awareness of the human body parts based on their experiences at home. They will already know quite a lot about the human life cycle, particularly if they have younger brothers or sisters (however, they may not be familiar with the term 'life cycle'). Many children will already have some ideas about health and healthy living, so be prepared to use this knowledge in early discussions.

By the end of Key Stage 1/Primary 3 (in Scotland) or Primary 4 (in Northern Ireland), children should be able to:

◆ use their knowledge about living things to describe basic conditions (such as a supply of food, water, air or light) that animals or plants need in order to survive;
◆ recognise that living things grow and reproduce;
◆ sort living things into groups using simple features, and describe the basis for their groupings;
◆ recognise that different living things are found in different places.

Preparing to use the poster

Whichever side of the poster you are using, make sure that all the children are able to see the poster clearly and to take part in all teaching and learning related to it. The poster must be displayed at an appropriate height to be easily accessible to the children (probably at the front of the room below the board), particularly for interactive display work. Check that any necessary additional materials (such as double-sided tape or labels) are available.

Other uses of the poster

In addition to its use in the activities in this book, the poster can be used as a resource for various purposes:

◆ counting activities (for example, *How many people are there? How many trees?*);

◆ naming and labelling activities (including work on spelling);

◆ discussion about what the characters are doing, what they will do next, and so on;

◆ sorting and classifying activities;

◆ a suitable wall display (as the backdrop).

LET'S LOOK AT THE POSTER

GROUP SIZE AND ORGANISATION
Whole class, sitting together on carpet area.
DURATION
15 minutes.
LEARNING OBJECTIVE
To explore and discuss the differences and similarities between living and non-living things, and between humans and other living things.

YOU WILL NEED
The colour 'people' poster, labels saying 'Living' and 'Non-living', Blu-Tack.

DISCUSSION QUESTIONS
Discuss the ideas of 'living' and 'non-living' with the children. Ask them whether they can say what makes a living thing different from something which is not living. Look at the poster with the children. Concentrate initially on the people (and thus implicitly on the children themselves) as living things.

Tell the children that all living animals breathe, feed, move, grow and make waste materials. (Reproduction and sensitivity will be too complex to explain at this stage, though later activities in this book deal with these topics.) Then ask the children whether they can think of any other things that living animals do. Expect responses such as 'make a noise', 'run' and possibly 'swim' and 'fly'.

Focus more directly on the poster and discuss questions such as:

◆ *Which of the living things in the poster are human?*

◆ *Which are animals?*

◆ *Which are plants?*

◆ *Which of the people are male? Which are female?*

◆ *Do you think they might belong to the same family? Why?*

◆ *Do you think they all come from the same country? Why?*

In raising these kinds of questions, you will be able to identify much about the children's awareness of many of the key concepts related to the subject:

◆ living and non-living;

◆ human and non-human;

◆ age and the life cycle;

◆ gender;

◆ family resemblance;

◆ ethnicity.

Ask the children to think about each of the items in the poster and consider whether it is living or non-living. Encourage them to explain their reasoning. Invite individuals to fix 'Living' and 'Non-living' labels onto appropriate parts of the poster, using Blu-Tack.

MY BODY

NAMES AND FUNCTIONS

GROUP SIZE AND ORGANISATION
Whole class, on chairs or seated on carpet. Teacher at front of class.
DURATION
About 25 minutes.
LEARNING OBJECTIVE
To be able to state the names and functions of the main external human body parts.

YOU WILL NEED
A list of actions (see below), the 'people' poster, body part labels photocopied from page 8 (preferably copied onto thin card and laminated), Blu-Tack.

WHAT TO DO
Organise the class as stated above, with enough space for the children to move their arms and legs freely. Start by leading the children in a sequence of basic 'follow the leader' type actions, where they need to move their limbs. Give clear and concise starting instructions, for example: *Do not move into someone else's space. Listen carefully to the instructions.*

Have a list ready with suitable actions to give the children experience of hearing the names of body parts. For example: *Lift up your arms. Wave your hands. Wiggle your fingers. Pat your head with your hand. Put both hands on your head. Stand on one leg. Stand on the other leg. Touch your knee. Touch your ankle. Touch your toes.* The timing for this will need to be carefully judged. The appropriate vocabulary to be used in this activity is given on photocopiable page 8.

When you decide that the children have had sufficient practice in this basic identification, sit them down and review the body part names. Now move on to work based on the 'people' poster. Start with a brief discussion about the poster and what it includes: animals, different people and so on. Then ask individual children to place the prepared labels correctly on any of the human figures shown in the poster. Each label, when correctly placed, can be attached to the poster.

As each label is attached, repeat the word(s) on it, point to the relevant body part on the poster and ask the children to point to the same part on their own bodies. Can they see any more examples of that body part on the poster? (For example, dogs have legs too.)

Encourage discussion by asking questions such as:
◆ *What do we use this body part for?*
◆ *What things can you do with your hands?*
◆ *What can you do with your legs?*
◆ *Do we all have the same main body parts?*
(Be sensitive to any disability in a child.)

A further possible development is to ask for two or three volunteers to stand perfectly still in front of the class. Repeat the labelling activity, with the labels being placed (using Blu-Tack) on the human 'models'.

ASSESSMENT
Using a simple class list on a grid, note the children who can easily name the relevant body parts and those who have difficulty and will need further help. Decide on a relatively high cut-off point for 'success', such as being able to name (and point out) nine out of ten main body parts.

IDEAS FOR DISPLAY
The 'people' poster could be displayed with the printed labels. The labels could be attached to the relevant body parts, or coloured strings could be used to connect each label to an appropriate body part.

IDEAS FOR DIFFERENTIATION
More confident children could produce their own written labels – or illustrated labels, with the correct word alongside a small drawing of the the body part – and attach these to the display. Some of the most able children could make their own drawings of the human body and label some of the parts.

OUTLINES

GROUP SIZE AND ORGANISATION
Groups of up to six children, working on the floor.
DURATION
About 30 minutes.
LEARNING OBJECTIVE
To reinforce knowledge of the names of the main external parts of the human body.

YOU WILL NEED
Large sheets or rolls of paper (this could be wallpaper, the 'reverse' side being used), thick marker pens or wax crayons, paints, a set of body part labels for each group (photocopied from page 8), newspapers.

MY BODY

WHAT TO DO

Tell the children that they are going to draw around each other, cut out the life-sized shapes, paint them and label the body parts using the names they have learned. Organise them into groups and give them the following instructions:

1. Lay out the sheet of paper on the floor.
2. Each group should select a child to lie still on top of the paper, while the others carefully draw around her or him.
3. The first child gets up, and another child cuts out the outline shape. (This will need to be managed carefully.)
4. Spread newspaper under the outline shape and paint the cut-out body carefully, showing the clothes and face.
5. When the paint is dry, stick the photocopied labels in place on the body.

Go round from group to group, supervising their work and assisting as necessary. Finally, encourage discussion of the finished paintings. You might ask the children: *Are the bodies made by each group the same, or are they different? How are they the same? How are they different?*

ASSESSMENT

Through careful observation, note exactly which body parts the children in each group are able to label confidently.

IDEAS FOR DISPLAY

The painted and labelled outlines can be mounted in a large display area to show a group of figures.

IDEAS FOR DIFFERENTIATION

Groups who are able to complete this activity quickly with one cut-out body could go on to produce a cut-out image of each child in the group, labelling it in new ways (for example, identifying the ankle, wrist, calf and thigh).

SIMILARITIES AND DIFFERENCES

GROUP SIZE AND ORGANISATION
Whole class.
DURATION
25 minutes.
LEARNING OBJECTIVE
To recognise similarities and differences between themselves and other children.

YOU WILL NEED

The 'people' poster, blank paper, pencils, a whiteboard/ flip chart and marker pen (or a chalkboard and chalk).

WHAT TO DO

Sit the children comfortably around the 'people' poster in a discussion group. Start the activity with a question: *Are we the same as the people in the poster?* Encourage discussion by asking the children to describe in what ways we are the same as the people in the poster. Responses may include: *We all have two legs. We all have a head. We all have a nose...*

Make brief notes on the board which highlight the similarities. Develop a clear definition of the word *same* with the children, and introduce the 'word *similar*.

Now ask the children to consider ways in which we are different from the people in the poster. Responses may include: *We are older than him. We have darker hair than her. We are shorter/thinner than him...*

Collect and note the differences on the board. Develop a clear definition of the word *difference* with the children. Choose two children and ask the class:
◆ *In what ways are they similar?*
◆ *In what ways are they different?*
Refer to the lists of similarities and differences on the board to help stimulate discussion.

Give each child a sheet of blank paper. Ask the children to draw two identical stick figures on the sheet (as in Figure 1). Now ask them to draw six things on each of the figures that are similar for both, and six things that are different.

ASSESSMENT

Check that the children are able to represent similarities and differences between two people on their stick figure drawings.

MY BODY

IDEAS FOR DISPLAY
The children could cut photographs of people out of magazines in order to put together a wall display showing similarities and differences.

IDEAS FOR DIFFERENTIATION
More confident children could explore similarities and differences between each other in greater depth, for example by making and recording measurements such as weight or height. Less confident children could explore differences and similarities between faces, looking at eye colour or hair colour in a group of children; they could find a pictorial way to illustrate their findings.

Figure I

MY FRIEND AND I

GROUP SIZE AND ORGANISATION
Pairs, sitting down.
DURATION
Ten minutes.
LEARNING OBJECTIVE
To recognise the similarities and differences between themselves and other children.

YOU WILL NEED
Photocopiable page 9, pencils, colouring pencils (or crayons), the 'people' poster (for reference).

WHAT TO DO
Arrange the children in working pairs and give each child a copy of photocopiable page 9. Review the definitions of *similar* and *different*.

Ask the children in each pair to look at each other, taking turns to say:
◆ *My friend and I are similar because...*
◆ *My friend and I are different because...*

Ask the children to illustrate the similarities and differences by drawing in the boxes on the photocopiable sheet, using the labels as prompts. Then ask them whether they can think of any other

similarities and differences which could be drawn in the unlabelled boxes.

Encourage careful observation reflected in clear, appropriately coloured illustration.

ASSESSMENT
Look for individual children successfully identifying similarities and differences between themselves and their friends.

IDEAS FOR DISPLAY
Choose two or three of the pairs and ask them to produce large, labelled pictures of themselves, highlighting the similarities and differences with labels.

IDEAS FOR DIFFERENTIATION
Encourage more confident children to look for less obvious similarities and differences, and to find appropriate ways of recording them. (For example: freckles, shape of eyebrows, shape of fingertips.) Less confident children could be given a version of photocopiable page 9 cut up to remove the unlabelled boxes.

THE SKELETON

GROUP SIZE AND ORGANISATION
Individuals.
DURATION
15 minutes.
LEARNING OBJECTIVE
To understand that the human body is supported by a framework of bones called the skeleton.

YOU WILL NEED
Photocopiable page 10 (enlarged to A3 size), the A2 skeleton poster; skeletons, fixing materials (Blu-Tack, adhesive or double-sided tape).

WHAT TO DO
Have the A2 skeleton poster displayed as a guide for the children to refer to. Give the children an A3 copy each of photocopiable page 10, scissors and fixing materials. Ask them to cut the sheet in half and look at the skeleton picture. Keep the teaching point very straightforward: *This is a picture of a skeleton. The skeleton is made up of lots of bones. It is the frame that supports your whole body. Everyone has a skeleton.*

RESOURCE
BANK

MY BODY

Now ask the children to cut out the body parts carefully from the 'Main body parts' picture and fix them onto the correct parts of the skeleton. Check the children's work and discuss any mistakes. Once the body parts are correctly fixed to the skeleton, the children can label them and colour them in.

ASSESSMENT
Look for success in placing the main external body parts over parts of the skeleton in the correct positions. In discussion, note which children are able to describe a skeleton as a frame made up of bones.

IDEAS FOR DISPLAY
The children's individual pictures of body parts arranged on a skeleton can be grouped around the skeleton poster. Children can be encouraged to draw and cut out body parts, then attach them to the skeleton poster.

IDEAS FOR DIFFERENTIATION
More confident children can go on to draw more detailed body parts, such as the neck, wrists and ankles, to fit onto the same or another skeleton shape. They should label these parts once they have placed them. Less confident children could be given the body parts already cut out and labelled, for them to fix in the correct positions.

ALL ABOUT MY BODY

GROUP SIZE AND ORGANISATION
Whole class.
DURATION
15 minutes.
LEARNING OBJECTIVE
To review the learning from the 'My body' section.

YOU WILL NEED
The A1 'people' poster, the A2 skeleton poster, photocopiable page 11, writing materials.

WHAT TO DO
Begin the lesson with a range of direct questions: *What is a living thing? Are we living things? What is a non-living thing? Can you name some other living things? Can you name some other non-living things?* Be sure to involve as many of the the children as possible. Then refer to the 'people' poster:
◆ *What are the living things on the poster?*
◆ *What are the non-living things on the poster?*
Ask the children to name the various external body parts. Develop this as a whole-class discussion: *Raise your arm... What is this called? What can it do?... Finally, ask: What is a skeleton? What does it do?* Refer to the skeleton poster, pointing out the various bones.

Finally, give out copies of photocopiable page 11. Encourage the children to complete this sheet as quickly as possible. They should use the words at the bottom of the sheet as prompts to help them label the body picture.

ASSESSMENT
In order to demonstrate success at this stage, the children need to be able to complete all of the sections on photocopiable page 11.

IDEAS FOR DISPLAY
At this point, the display can take the form of a class presentation in (for example) an assembly. Let the children think of ways to demonstrate what they know about their bodies. They could use the 'people' poster and display the materials they have completed as part of their presentation.

IDEAS FOR DIFFERENTIATION
More confident children could use the reverse side of photocopiable page 11 to list the names and functions of various body parts from memory. In addition, ask them to draw the basic skeleton (in pencil) onto the 'My body' picture.

Give less confident children specific instructions related to the 'My body' sheet – for example: *colour the arms red, colour the legs blue.* This will give you a clear indication of the childrens' familiarity with the names and positions of the main external body parts.

Body part labels

eye	hair	arm
head	hand	elbow
nose	leg	mouth
foot	trunk	knee
ankle	ear	finger
toe	neck	wrist

PHOTOCOPIABLE
RESOURCE
BANK

MY BODY

Name _____   Date _____

My friend and I

My friend's name is:

We are similar because:

two hands	two feet	head	legs
arms	nose	mouth	ears

◆Any other similarities?

We are different because:

hair colour	eye colour	size	shape
fingerprints	height	weight	shoe size

◆Any other differences?

PHOTOCOPIABLE
RESOURCE
BANK

MY BODY

Name _____   Date _____

Body parts

◆ Fix the body parts onto this skeleton.

Skeleton

◆ Cut out these body parts and fix them onto the skeleton.

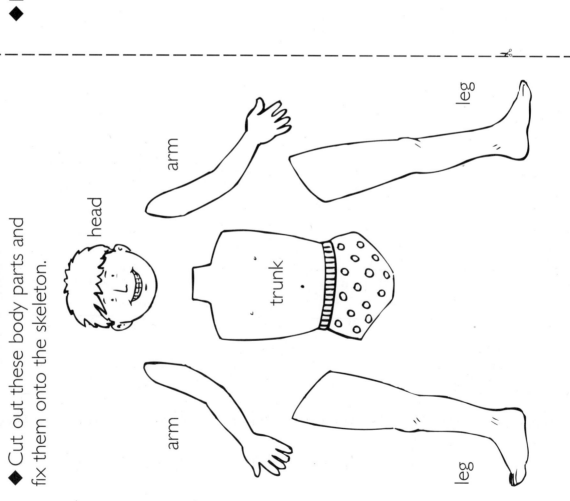

head

arm

leg

trunk

arm

leg

Name _____   Date _____

My body

I am a __ __ __ __ __ __ thing.

◆ Name the body parts.

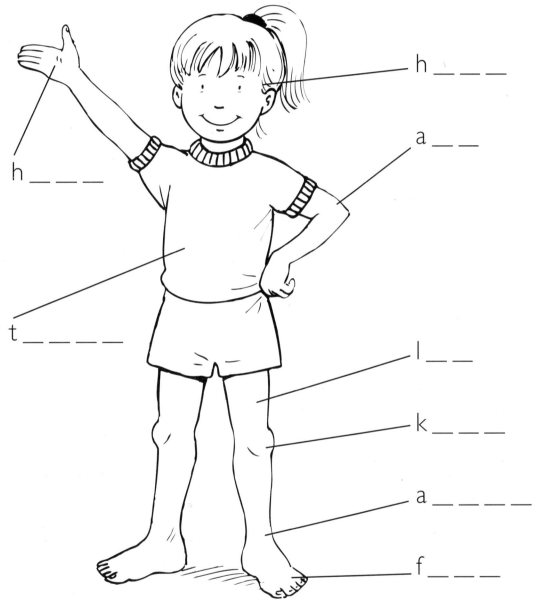

h _ _ _

a _ _

h _ _ _ _

t _ _ _ _ _

l _ _

k _ _ _ _

a _ _ _ _ _

f _ _ _

The frame of
the body is the s _ _ _ _ _ _ _ _ _.

Words you need: skeleton   leg   head   ankle   hand

                    trunk   living   knee   arm   foot

MY SENSES

FIVE SENSES

GROUP SIZE AND ORGANISATION
Whole class.
DURATION
30 minutes.
LEARNING OBJECTIVE
To understand that humans have five senses which enable them to be aware of the world around them, and that these operate through the sense organs.

YOU WILL NEED
The 'people' poster, a whiteboard/flip chart and marker pen (or a chalkboard and chalk), photocopiable page 15, scissors, adhesive, coloured pencils or crayons, simple individual outline drawings of the nose, ears, eyes, hand and tongue.

WHAT TO DO
Start a class discussion with the question: *What are the senses?* Invite a range of responses, noting them on the board. Sort the responses according to sense, and tell the children that they have five senses.

Display the outline drawings one by one, starting with the eye. Ask the children: *What is this a picture of? What do you do with them?* Through discussion, elicit the response: *You see with your eyes.* Continue through the five outline drawings, in each case adding a new sentence: *You hear with your ears. You smell with your nose. You taste with your tongue. You touch with your fingers.* Use repetition to emphasise these ideas.

Now use the 'people' poster as a basis for questions relating to the senses – for example:
◆ *Is anyone in the picture touching anything?*
◆ *What do you think the people can hear?*
Take each of the senses in turn and ask the class a range of questions to stimulate discussion:
◆ *What can you see?*
◆ *Can you hear any sounds?*
◆ *What would you like to taste at lunchtime?*
◆ *What on your desk feels smooth? What feels rough?*
◆ *What is your favourite smell?*
Continue in this vein, giving the children a range of opportunities to use and discuss their five senses. Be prepared for a fairly 'excited' set of responses! Also, be aware of any child whose vision or hearing is impaired.

Ask the children how they think their senses can help to keep them safe. Encourage responses related to crossing the road carefully, listening to instructions, not touching hot things in the kitchen and so on.

Give each child a copy of photocopiable page 15. Ask them to cut out the shapes from the bottom of the page carefully, and to place them on the head outline. To add a different slant to the task, ask them to put all the shapes in the wrong places and then swap their sheet with a partner, who can try to position them correctly. This will help to establish how well they understand the positions of the sense organs. Now ask them to stick the shapes in place and to write the correct senses in the label spaces. Finally, they can colour in the face.

Extend the activity by asking the children to make up a 'listening chart' for the sounds they hear at home. They could write down, or mark against a list, the different sounds they hear in a given amount of time. The children can then devise ways to show this information in a diagram or picture.

ASSESSMENT
In a whole-class discussion activity of this kind, formal assessment can be difficult. However, it should be possible to note which children are fully aware of their senses and which are less sure. The children's completed sheets will indicate whether they know the positions and functions of the sense organs.

IDEAS FOR DISPLAY
Ask the children to collect or draw a picture related to each of the senses. These could be cut out of magazines. The collected pictures can be stuck down in a frieze beside each of the sense organ outline drawings. For example, pictures of food could be put alongside the tongue or the nose. A range of different textured materials could also feature beside the hand for touch. The children could write large clear labels for the five senses (or print them using a word processor) to add to the frieze.

MY SENSES

IDEAS FOR DIFFERENTIATION

More confident children could produce their own outline drawings of the sense organs, and list some of the things they can detect with each sense. Ask them to find a way to show the sense of touch in the drawing on photocopiable page 15. They might choose to add hands below the face; or to show a finger against the skin of the face.

Less confident children could take part in a practical reinforcement activity in which they move in response to statements. For example, when you say 'We smell with our...', the children should point to their noses. Progress through the senses several times, changing the order and speeding up to encourage quick recall. The children could also be given page 15 with the sense organs already cut out and fixed in the wrong places; the children then have to reposition them.

WHICH SENSE?

GROUP SIZE AND ORGANISATION
Groups of 4 to 6 children.
DURATION
20 minutes.
LEARNING OBJECTIVE
To understand that humans have senses which enable them to be aware of the world around them.

YOU WILL NEED
Photocopiable page 16, scissors, adhesive, crayons.

WHAT TO DO
Arrange the children into groups; then give each child a copy of photocopiable page 16. Ask them to cut out the small pictures at the bottom of the sheet. Then encourage them (working individually) to place the pictures in the correct sense boxes.

Wait until everyone has used up all 15 of the small pictures. Ask the children in each group to explain to each other why they have placed each picture on a particular sense. Discuss any differences of opinion that arise. For example, the rain could be 'see', 'hear' or 'feel'. Encourage the children to talk about how some things stimulate more than one sense.

ASSESSMENT
Note which children are able to sort the pictures appropriately and explain the thinking behind their choices. The level of reasoning behind the choice of senses is a clear indication of the child's ability.

IDEAS FOR DISPLAY

The 'Senses game' sheet could be enlarged to A3 and placed on a table as an interactive display. The collection of pictures to be sorted could be expanded using drawings or photographs cut out of magazines. Children could be encouraged to note their choices on a simple tally chart as part of the display.

IDEAS FOR DIFFERENTIATION

More confident children could add different sets of pictures (which they have drawn or cut from other sources) to their game.

For less confident children, the game could be colour-coded. The sense pictures could each be a different colour, with the small pictures coloured to match the senses. Where there is a potential mixture of senses, the small picture could show two or three colours and the child will need to make a choice.

SENSES SURVEY

GROUP SIZE AND ORGANISATION
Groups of 4 to 6.
DURATION
10 minutes.
LEARNING OBJECTIVE
To understand that humans have senses which enable them to be aware of the world around them.

YOU WILL NEED
Photocopiable page 17, pencils, crayons.

WHAT TO DO
Arrange the children into groups. Give each child a copy of photocopiable page 17. Ask them to write down or sketch, quickly, the things they have used their senses for so far that day. Limit the time for this to two or three minutes.

See who in each group has recorded the most items. Rearrange the groups so that the children in each group have found the same number. Give the children another two or three minutes to record more items. Collect the total numbers of different items from each group, record them on a tally chart and plot them on a bar chart (as in Figure 2).

MY SENSES

Figure 2. Tally and Bar Chart

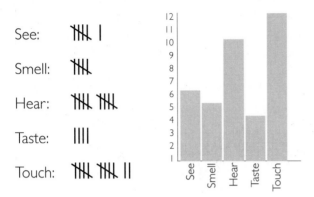

See: IIII I

Smell: IIII

Hear: IIII IIII

Taste: IIII

Touch: IIII IIII II

It will now be possible for the children to identify which of the senses has been used the most and least in the whole class. The results may provide opportunities for questioning – for example:

◆ *Why have you used this sense so much today?*
◆ *Is the result likely to be the same every day?*
◆ *Why have you used one of the senses less than all the others?*
◆ *Do you use any of the senses at special times in the day, more than at other times?*

ASSESSMENT
Note which children are able to identify the five senses (from the sense organ pictures) and indicate clearly when they might be used.

IDEAS FOR DIFFERENTIATION
More confident children could be encouraged to choose how to display their data, using a range of methods. Less confident children could display their data using boxes filled with different colours, leading directly towards a bar chart.

SENSES REVIEW

GROUP SIZE AND ORGANISATION
Whole class.
DURATION
15 minutes.
LEARNING OBJECTIVE
To review the learning from the 'My senses' section.

YOU WILL NEED
The 'people' poster, labels of the senses ('Touch', 'See', 'Hear', 'Taste', 'Smell'), labels of the sensory organs ('Eyes', 'Tongue', 'Ears', 'Nose', 'Skin'), Blu-Tack.

WHAT TO DO
Spread out the labels on a table. Ask the children which sense organ is responsible for seeing; then ask a child to attach the 'See' label and the 'Eyes' label to an appropriate place on the poster. Progress through the five senses, choosing different children to position the labels each time.

Now ask the children to say whether the labels could be fixed in other places on the poster, and to explain why (for example, 'Because dogs have ears too'). Invite responses, then ask individual children to move the labels to other appropriate positions on the main poster. Each time, reinforce the concepts by asking the children to repeat the name of the relevant sense and sense organ and its position.

ASSESSMENT
Through discussion during and after the activity, note which children are fully aware of the five main senses, the related sense organs and their main locations on the body.

IDEAS FOR DISPLAY
The labelled poster can be left in an accessible place for the children to move the labels or add to them as they wish. This kind of interactive, non-static display can become an effective tool for reinforcement.

IDEAS FOR DIFFERENTIATION
To develop their understanding of the senses further, children could be asked to complete a survey at home. For example, they could perform a taste survey based on their meals for the day, using the headings 'Sweet', 'Sour', 'Salty', 'Bitter', 'Spicy' and/or others; or a smell survey based on cleaning, cooking and so on.

NB When they are involved in any activity involving tasting and smelling, make sure that you are aware of any allergic reactions the children may exhibit. Nut allergies, in particular, can be very dangerous; wheat products and some fruits also commonly cause allergic reactions. If you are in any doubt, always check with parents or carers before setting up such an activity.

Less confident children could be given more opportunities to move the sense labels around. Individual children can be given copies of the labels and encouraged to turn the activity into a timed game. How quickly can they use up all of their labels? Can they place their labels where no-one else has?

MY SENSES

Name —————————————— Date ——————————————

Fixing the senses

taste		hear
see		smell

s		h
s		t

◆ Cut out the shapes and fix them in place.
◆ Which ones cannot be used? Why not?

touch

ear	eye	nose	hand

tongue	ear	eye	fingers

MY SENSES

Senses game

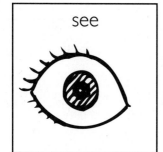

see

hear

smell

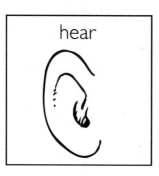

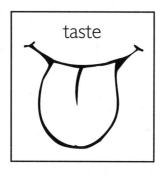

taste

touch

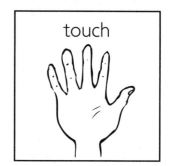

◆ Cut out the pictures below.
Put each one on the correct sense picture.

rainbow	drum	sweets	horse	light bulb
egg and bacon	trumpet	book	bell	paint
pencil	guitar	dog barking	sunshine	rain

ME AND MY BODY

MY SENSES

Senses survey

How many things have you used your senses for today?

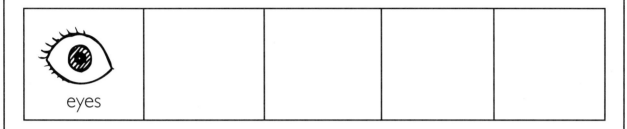

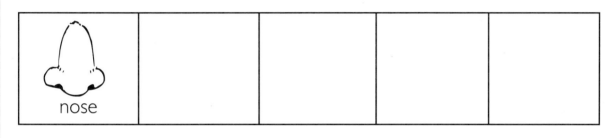

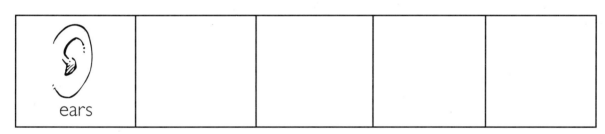

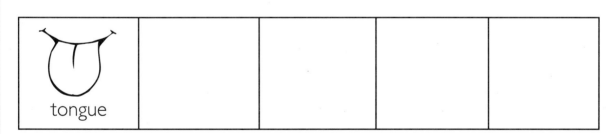

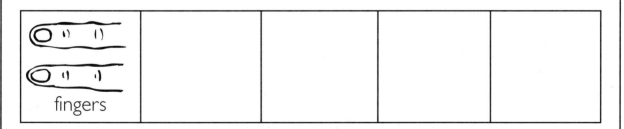

◆ Fill in the boxes, then turn over for more spaces.

HEALTHY LIVING

A DAY IN THE LIFE

GROUP SIZE AND ORGANISATION
Whole class.
DURATION
30 minutes.
LEARNING OBJECTIVE
To understand that taking exercise and eating the right kinds of food keep us healthy.

YOU WILL NEED
The A2 poster 'A day in the life', pencils or crayons, three small pieces of paper per child (to fit the blank spaces on the poster).

WHAT TO DO
Talk to the children about the activities that make up your own typical day. Include details such as getting up, mealtimes and other regular routines.

Invite individual children to talk about their typical day. What has happened to them today since they woke up? Are they able to put times to all their activities? Highlight the activities that are related to eating or exercise (probably most of them).

Show the children the 'A day in the life' black and white poster. Explain that it represents twelve hours in a day. Take them around the clock, starting with the hour just before the time of the first lesson that day (for example, if your first lesson is at 9.15, start with 9.00). Point to each of the blank spaces on the poster, asking: *What do we do at this time?* Encourage responses such as: *9.00 we start school, 10.00 we do reading, 11.00 we play outside...*

When you have got back to your starting point, ask the children what happens *then* in a real day. Some children will be able to tell you that the next 12 hours are night-time. Work around (pointing to the inside edge of the clock face) until you reach your original starting point; then recap the daily routines.

Give each child three small pieces of paper. Ask the children to draw and colour in a morning, afternoon and evening activity. Help them to decide on a time (to the nearest hour) for each activity and write the times on the drawings. When the drawings are finished, attach a selection to the poster (in the blank spaces). Ask the children to sort the unused drawings into piles according to time (9.00, 10.00 and so on), and to arrange these piles in a circle.

Discuss with the children which of the activity drawings relate to food, and which relate to exercise. Mark the relevant drawings with different-coloured dots. Remind them of what was said earlier about the food- and exercise-related activities in a typical day. Ask them to discuss these activities, leading them towards the idea that food gives us the energy to do other things. For example, eating breakfast helps us to work and play during the morning; by lunchtime we are tired and hungry again.

ASSESSMENT
Note which children are able to order the times and identify what they are doing at different times of the day; and which children can go on to relate the activities to food and exercise.

IDEAS FOR DISPLAY
Display the 'A day in the life' poster at child height. Allow the children to take turns at various times to change the pictures on the clock for others in the piles. The space inside the clock could be filled with a collage of the children's illustrations.

IDEAS FOR DIFFERENTIATION
More confident children could draw small clock faces showing the times on their activity pictures. The pictures could then be used for a sequencing exercise. The children could then consider how to show the full 24 hours of the day. Less confident children could try to sort the pictures according to various criteria: school time/home time, play/work and so on.

LIVING THINGS AND US

GROUP SIZE AND ORGANISATION
Groups of 4 to 6.
DURATION
15 minutes.
LEARNING OBJECTIVE
To learn about the common links between living things.

YOU WILL NEED
The 'people' poster, photocopiable page 23, scissors, coloured pens or crayons, large sheets (one per group) of coloured sugar paper divided into four labelled sections (see Figure 3).

Figure 3

Move	Eat
Breathe	Grow

WHAT TO DO

Arrange the children into groups. Give each child a copy of photocopiable page 23; give each group a piece of labelled backing paper. Ask the children to write their names on each of the small pictures, colour them and cut them out carefully along the dotted lines.

Next, the children in each group should take turns to place their pictures on the backing paper under whichever headings they think are most appropriate. Try to encourage the children to think for themselves rather than copy the person who goes first. When they have all placed their pictures, encourage discussion about their choices. Try to raise their awareness that each of the pictures can be placed correctly under more than one heading.

Ask individual children to describe the common links between the living things. For example: *The daffodil grows... we grow. The dog moves... the fly moves.* If appropriate, explain that living plants make food in their leaves using air and sunlight, and that air passes into and out of the leaves. Alternatively, let the children assume that only animals eat and breathe.

Now ask the children in each group to work together, placing their pictures so that under 'Move' they will have all the pictures of living things that move (ie animals), and so on.

Finally, look at the 'people' poster with the children. Can they see examples of living things moving, eating, breathing and growing?

ASSESSMENT

Note which children are able to discuss, and show using pictures, what living things have in common.

IDEAS FOR DISPLAY

The groups' completed 'Living things and us' charts can be displayed. Pictures of further living things could be cut from magazines, labelled and added to the charts.

IDEAS FOR DIFFERENTIATION

More confident children can develop their display charts by drawing and labelling further living things on them. They could also look at some of the other characteristics of living things, such as reproduction and getting rid of waste, and add these to the chart. For less confident children, the display chart could be limited to two factors (such as 'Eat' and 'Grow').

EATING

GROUP SIZE AND ORGANISATION
Whole-class discussion, then individual research.
DURATION
20–30 minutes for discussion, research over weekend, 15 minutes for follow-up work.
LEARNING OBJECTIVE
To understand that eating the right kinds and amounts of food helps us to keep healthy.

YOU WILL NEED

A letter to parents or carers (see below), food survey sheets (see below), writing materials, a whiteboard and marker pen (or chalkboard and chalk).

WHAT TO DO

Send a letter to the children's parents or carers, asking for support in collecting data about what the children eat over a typical weekend (Saturday and Sunday). Prepare two 'food survey sheets' for each child: A4 sheets labelled 'Saturday' and 'Sunday', each sheet divided into six boxes.

Talk to the children about the food they (and you) eat on a daily basis. Be careful to use whatever vocabulary is appropriate and understandable to them (for example, avoid confusion between *tea*, *dinner* and *supper*). Discuss with them what makes up a balanced diet. Use the words *proteins*, *vitamins*, *minerals*, *carbohydrates*, *fats* and *fibre* as list headings on the board. Explain these headings in simple terms, and list some common foods under each heading:
◆ Vitamins and minerals, eg vegetables, fruit, milk. Special chemicals needed (in small amounts) for our bodies to work properly.
◆ Carbohydrates, eg bread, potatoes, rice. The main source of energy for exercise.

HEALTHY LIVING

◆ Proteins, eg fish, meat, beans, milk. Needed for growth and repair.

◆ Fats, eg cheese, meat. Small amounts needed for energy and keeping warm.

◆ Fibre, eg bread, fruit, cereals. Needed to help us digest food.

Refer to the term 'energy' in its scientific sense: the power or ability of someone or something to do physical work. Help the children to realise that they get the energy they use during the day by eating food. Explain in simple terms that food is a kind of fuel that keeps us moving. Make the point that, in general, there is no such thing as 'good' foods and 'bad' foods; but there are *healthy and unhealthy diets* which we need to find out about. The body needs a healthy diet so that it can grow and work properly.

Give the children copies of the prepared survey sheets. Ask them to fill these in with their parents during the next weekend. (**NB** When setting a 'homework' task in this way, be sensitive to the fact that many children are tired at the end of the week, and that some children may not receive appropriate support for doing homework.)

In a follow-up session, help the children to categorise the foods they have listed on their survey sheets. Encourage them to see how their everyday diet contains a mixture of different kinds of foods.

ASSESSMENT

Note which children are able to highlight the kinds of foods they have eaten and produce appropriate data to show this.

IDEAS FOR DISPLAY

The children's completed surveys could be displayed to show the range of foods eaten. Collections of food pictures cut from magazines and packaging, and classified under the scientific names *proteins, fibre, fats, carbohydrates, vitamins* and *minerals*, can be made into a large wall collage.

IDEAS FOR DIFFERENTIATION

More confident children could collect information from other children about what they eat, and find ways to represent it. They might use bar charts, pictograms and so on. They could then try to sort the foods into the correct scientific groups (proteins, fats and so on). They could also go on to explore the idea of a balanced, healthy diet.

Less confident children could group their findings under more obvious headings, such as *hot food/cold food* or *main meal/snack*. They could collect data from other children to group under these headings.

EXERCISE

GROUP SIZE AND ORGANISATION
Whole class, then individuals.
DURATION
20 minutes for discussion, research over evening, 15 minutes for follow-up work.
LEARNING OBJECTIVE
To understand that we need to take regular exercise in order to keep healthy.

YOU WILL NEED
Photocopiable page 24, pencils.

WHAT TO DO
Tell the children about exercise: *Exercise is a very important part of living. It helps to keep you fit and healthy. If you don't exercise, you will become weak and ill.* Discuss some different types of exercise. Start with a series of questions such as:

◆ *Who has done some running today?*
◆ *Who can ride a bike? Who can swim?*
◆ *What sorts of exercise can you do every day?*
◆ *What sorts of exercise do you enjoy most?*

Go on to tell the children that when they exercise, their hearts will beat faster and they might get out of breath. If your science lesson can be linked with a PE activity, the children will enjoy proving this: ask them to run around for a couple of minutes, then stop and see how they feel. Can they feel their hearts beating faster? Are they breathing faster? (**NB** Avoid inflicting any distress on children who may be unfit.)

Give each child a copy of photocopiable page 24. Ask them to draw pictures of the different kinds of exercise they have had during the day so far. Ask them to take the sheet home and fill in whatever types of exercise they do outside school. (**NB** When setting a 'homework' task in this way, be sensitive to the fact that many children are tired at the end of the day, and that some children may not receive appropriate support for doing homework.)

When the children have completed their sheets, use their results to collate an overall list or chart. The children can then look at the overall results and complete some data handling work, answering questions such as *How many children rode bikes?* or *How many children went running?*

ASSESSMENT
Note which children are able to record and discuss information about exercise, and show awareness

(through discussion) of the effect that regular exercise will have on their bodies.

IDEAS FOR DISPLAY
Make a class exercise chart, using squared paper. Ask the children to colour in a square each time they do a particular type of exercise (such as running).

Ask the children to collect pictures (from magazines or swap cards) of professional sports players or athletes in action, and to label each picture with the type of exercise ('running', 'swimming' and so on). The pictures can be used to make up a collage.

IDEAS FOR DIFFERENTIATION
Children who are confident both in taking exercise and in carrying out investigations can start to explore their heartbeat in more detail. They can work in pairs, with appropriate supervision, to measure their pulse rate before and after some exercise.

Less confident children could carry out a basic survey of the exercise taken regularly by their parents or carers. For example, do they go running? Do they go to a gym? Do they ride a bicycle? This information can be collated by the teacher and displayed on a bar chart or a pictogram.

MEDICINES AT HOME

GROUP SIZE AND ORGANISATION
Whole class, then individuals.
DURATION
30 minutes.
LEARNING OBJECTIVE
To learn about drugs as medicines.

YOU WILL NEED
Pictures of some common children's medicines (perhaps from a chemist's shop; include pictures of paracetamol tablets, asthma inhalers, cough mixture and antiseptic cream or spray), empty packets and boxes of common children's medicines, photocopiable page 25, writing materials.

WHAT TO DO
Firstly, and most importantly, tell the children that they should never touch any medicine without an adult knowing.

Explain clearly that sometimes when you are ill, you will need medicine. Some medicines are liquids to drink, some are pills to be swallowed and others are creams or ointments to rub onto the body. Also, point out that some medicines are given by injection. Show the children the pictures and containers of common 'child' medicines, asking whether the children have seen these before.

There may well be children in the class who regularly use asthma medication; take this opportunity to explain to the others what this is and why many children need it. Some of the children may also currently be taking prescription medicines such as antibiotics. Explain what the word *prescription* means: the doctor gives a prescription to take to the chemist, and it gives details of the amount of a particular medicine needed.

Give each child a copy of photocopiable page 25, and explain carefully how the children are to use it. Ask them to take the sheet home and, with the help of a parent or carer, to tick the medicines they have in their homes. When the children return to school with their completed photocopiable sheets, collate the information for display.

ASSESSMENT
Note (in discussion) which children are aware that medicines have a role in helping to keep us fit and free from illness.

IDEAS FOR DISPLAY
The children's findings can be collated and displayed as a bar chart, alongside some of the materials collected from the chemist.

IDEAS FOR DIFFERENTIATION
More confident children can fill in the bottom of the photocopiable sheet with drawings of other 'child' medicines found in the home (with adult help).

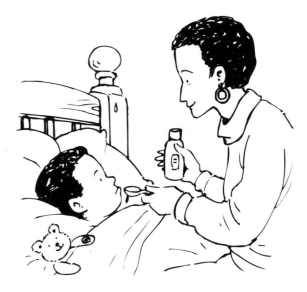

Alternatively, they could find and cut out magazine advertisements to redraw. Some children may be able to plan and carry out a survey of what medicines are currently being taken in the class (and by how many children). This data could then be displayed on bar charts or pictograms.

Less confident children could look more closely at the pictures and containers provided. They can study the labels, looking for clues that these medicines are intended for children – for example, the type of illustration on the packaging or the words used.

LIVING SAFELY

GROUP SIZE AND ORGANISATION
Whole class.
DURATION
20 minutes.
LEARNING OBJECTIVE
To explore ways of living safely and to be aware of possible dangers.

YOU WILL NEED
Examples of danger signs and warning notices (warnings on containers of household cleaning chemicals, pictures of road warning signs and so on), a whiteboard or flip chart and marker pen (or a chalkboard and chalk), paper and drawing materials.

WHAT TO DO
With any work on a theme of this nature, it is often best to involve the children's parents or carers in the planning of it, so that they will be able to follow it up at home if they wish. It might be appropriate to write a note to parents or carers to inform them of the overall theme of this piece of work.

This lesson will be primarily a class discussion, so arrange the children in such a way that they will feel comfortable in responding to questions. Write the following headings on the board:

At home   At school

    Coming to school   Others

Ask the children to think about each heading in turn and to suggest possible dangers which should be listed under each heading. For example, under 'At home', they might list:
◆ Dangers in the kitchen such as hot cooking rings, oven and kettle.
◆ Dangers in the bathroom such as cleaning materials and unknown medicines.

Show the children some examples of the type of labelling found on products which could be harmful to them. Discuss the point of this labelling, and draw out the conclusion that the safest approach is not to touch anything that might present any danger to them.

Ask the children to tell you about the dangers that they have to be aware of every day. When might these dangers arise? For example, traffic is a danger when they are crossing the road; strangers may be a danger when they are walking to school. Draw up a reasonably comprehensive list of potential dangers which the children might be facing regularly.

Ask the children to think about how they will ensure their own safety. With their help, devise a set of rules for safe living. Write these out for display in the classroom. It might be useful for each child to take a copy of the safety rules home.

As a follow-up, it may be possible to take the children to a display or event on the theme of safety provided by a local organisation; or an organisation may be able to send someone to visit the school in order to talk to the children about personal safety. For example, you might like to approach the local community police officer or the RoSPA.

ASSESSMENT
Make sure that all the children are developing a safety-conscious attitude.

IDEAS FOR DISPLAY
Ask the children to create 'Be Safe!' posters. These could focus on any aspect of the work covered. The completed posters will be valuable display materials for use in the classroom and elsewhere in the school.

IDEAS FOR DIFFERENTIATION
More confident children will be able to think of and write their own lists of 'safe rules' – for example, rules for using the playground or the PE apparatus safely. They can add pictures to highlight important issues.

Less confident children could use a cassette recorder to record their tips for safety in particular situations (for example, in the playground). The 'safety tape' could be used alongside the 'safe rules' and posters from the other groups, and the whole theme of living safely could be presented in class or in a school assembly.

Living things and us

us	worm	daffodil
Name _____	Name _____	Name _____
tree	dog	fly
Name _____	Name _____	Name _____
robin	fish	mushroom
Name _____	Name _____	Name _____

PHOTOCOPIABLE
RESOURCE
BANK

HEALTHY LIVING

Name _____   Date _____

Exercise diary

Did you run, jump, walk, climb, swim, throw, hop, skip?

◆ Draw pictures to show all the kinds of exercise you had today.

ME AND MY BODY

HEALTHY LIVING

Name _____   Date _____

Medicines at home

Do you have any of these?

◆ Find out by asking at home.

Yes   No

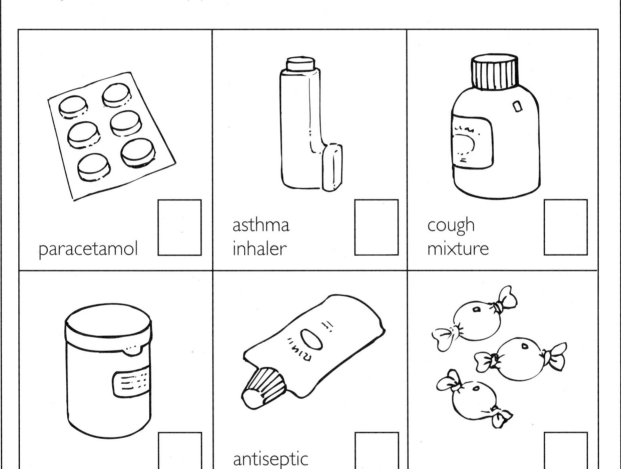

| paracetamol | asthma inhaler | cough mixture |
| antibiotic | antiseptic cream | cough sweets |

◆ Do you have any other medicines for children?

THE LIFE CYCLE

GROWING UP

GROUP SIZE AND ORGANISATION
Whole class.
DURATION
20 minutes.
LEARNING OBJECTIVES
To explore their own knowledge about growing up.
To become aware of their part in the human life cycle.

YOU WILL NEED
The 'people' poster, a large sheet of paper (or flip chart) and marker pens, photocopiable page 30, coloured pens or crayons, adhesive.

WHAT TO DO
With the children, look again at the 'people' poster. Point out the illustrations from it which highlight the different stages of the life cycle: baby, child, adult, older adult. Introduce and explain the term 'life cycle': the different stages of a living thing's life, including how it produces 'children'.

Ask the children whether they have any brothers or sisters. If so, who is the oldest/youngest? Work together to identify who in the class has the youngest and the oldest brother or sister. Plot the information onto a bar chart.

Ask whether the children who have younger brothers or sisters can remember when their brother or sister was very tiny, or even before he/she was born. What can they remember about the baby? Collect and share ideas. Most young children will know that the baby grows inside the mother. Using the correct vocabulary, tell the children that the baby grows inside its mother's womb and that this takes nine months.

Ask the children what they think happens to the mother as the baby grows. Perhaps a pregnant mother related to one of the children could be invited to visit the class and talk (in fairly simple terms) about what is happening to her body.

Give each child a copy of photocopiable page 30. This sheet can be filled in during the lesson or at home, as appropriate. Ideally, the children should collect photographs from home to stick in the four spaces; beside each photo, they should write in the age of the person when the photo was taken. Alternatively, they could draw pictures in the spaces, perhaps with some help from their parents at home.

Be particularly sensitive about this work with children who may not have living grandparents. If appropriate, the heading can be changed to 'Older relatives' or 'Older friends'. Also, discuss the fact that some children may be brought up by foster-parents. Explain that foster-parents are not the natural parents, and that there will be little family resemblance. Take care with this issue, using tact and sensitivity.

ASSESSMENT
From discussion of the photocopiable sheet, note which children are aware of their position in the life cycle compared to a baby, an adult and an older person.

IDEAS FOR DISPLAY
The photos or drawings provided by the children can be used to make up an entertaining display. They can either be labelled to identify the individuals or left with question marks so that others can guesss who is who. (NB Remember to obtain parental permission if the photos are going to be displayed.) The theme can be developed by asking colleagues to provide photos of themselves when they were children.

IDEAS FOR DIFFERENTIATION
More confident children can use the ages written alongside the photos to work out each person's year of birth, and to answer questions such as: *Who is the youngest person represented in all the photos? Who is the oldest?*

Less confident children could use the photos for a sequencing activity: arranging them in order of age. They should start with the youngest person and work up to the oldest, then try to reverse the order. Working in small groups, they could discuss similarities and differences between the people featured in the photos.

RESOURCE BANK

ME AND MY BODY

THE LIFE CYCLE

FIRST STAGE

GROUP SIZE AND ORGANISATION
Whole class and groups of 4 to 6.
DURATION
20 minutes.
LEARNING OBJECTIVE
To understand that they began life as a small baby, and that this was the first stage of their life cycle outside the mother's body.

YOU WILL NEED
Photographs collected of the children as babies (see 'Growing up').

WHAT TO DO
Remind the children what a 'life cycle' is, and where they are in terms of the human life cycle.

Working in groups, the children can look at the photos of themselves and their classmates as babies. Give them time to discuss the similarities and differences they can see between the photos, and how much they have changed since the photos were taken.

Explain to the children about twins, triplets and other multiple births. Then explain (in simple terms) about premature births. Some of the children may know that they were born prematurely. Talk about the food that babies are able to eat: how they start with milk, either from the mother's breast or from special powder in bottles.

Talk about how the baby learns by using its senses to become aware of the outside world. Remind the children about their first day at school. Ask the children to find ways to record or illustrate their earliest memories. These could include pictures, brief written accounts and pieces scribed by an adult.

ASSESSMENT
Note which children are aware of the first stage of the human life cycle, and their own position within the life cycle.

IDEAS FOR DISPLAY
See 'Growing up' (page 26).

IDEAS FOR DIFFERENTIATION
More confident children can be encouraged to develop written and illustrated accounts of their earliest memories into stories, perhaps incorporating fictional elements (for example, the earliest memories of a child born in another part of the world).

Less confident children could use a cassette recorder to record their thoughts and ideas about babies. You could then scribe the text onto large sheets for display purposes. The children could cut appropriate pictures out of magazines to illustrate the human life cycle, arranging them in a sequence.

GETTING OLDER

GROUP SIZE AND ORGANISATION
Whole class, then groups of 4 to 6.
DURATION
20 minutes.
LEARNING OBJECTIVE
To be aware of the changes in the middle years of the human life cycle.

YOU WILL NEED
The 'people' poster, large sheets of paper (one per group) folded to give four sections, unbreakable plastic mirrors, coloured pens or crayons.

WHAT TO DO
Focus the children's attention on the 'people' poster. Discuss how the older people differ from the children, and in what ways they appear to be the same.

Ask the children in what ways they are similar to their parents. For example, do they have the same eye colour or hair colour? Talk about the changes that can occur as people become adults – for example, men can grow facial hair.

Organise the children into groups. Give out the folded sheets of paper and ask the children to label the sections as shown in Figure 4. Discuss how they should work out the ages. For example, if they are currently six years old, they can practice adding on in lots of 10 to reach 16, 26 and 36 years old. Can they see a pattern in the numbers when adding on in 10s?

Encourage the groups to discuss what they think they will look like 10, 20 and 30 years from now. Allow the children plenty of time for this discussion, as they

THE LIFE CYCLE

will enjoy sharing their ideas and may not have a particularly clear idea of how long 10 or 20 years will be – all 'grown-ups' are 'old' to them. Explain the difference between being 'mature' and being 'old'.

Representatives of each group could report on their ideas to the rest of the class before the children start to draw pictures on their sheets. The initial picture 'Me now, aged _____' should be as detailed as possible. Encourage the children to use plastic mirrors to focus on particular facial features. As they draw the pictures, they should pay attention to the details of faces and clothing. They could add what they consider to be appropriate accessories to the pictures.

To conclude the lesson, the children can review and share their ideas and illustrations with others in the class.

Figure 4

Me now, aged _____	Me in 10 years, aged _____
Me in 20 years, aged _____	Me in 30 years, aged _____

ASSESSMENT
Note which children are able to represent their own likely development in the middle years of the life cycle with accuracy.

IDEAS FOR DISPLAY
The pictures produced by the children could form an impressive display, especially if a sample of the pictures showing each age group (or of the pictures drawn by each group of children) were enlarged on the photocopier. This would allow you to select the best of many individual efforts. The enlarged photocopies could be coloured in by hand.

IDEAS FOR DIFFERENTIATION
More confident children could develop this idea by drawing pictures of how they might look 40 or 50 years from now. In addition, they could use descriptive writing to annotate the pictures. They may find it interesting to put their pictures alongside any photographs of parents, grandparents and older relatives to promote discussion about likenesses in family groups.

Children who are less clear about what getting older entails could try to imagine how they might look when they are adults, instead of attempting to imagine themselves at specific ages.

THE CIRCLE GAME

GROUP SIZE AND ORGANISATION
Whole-class or group discussion; paired activity.
DURATION
15 minutes.
LEARNING OBJECTIVE
To be able to arrange all the stages of the human life cycle in a sequence.

YOU WILL NEED
Photocopiable pages 31 and 32 (cut out the game cards in advance), coloured counters, a dice.

WHAT TO DO
Explain the rules of the game to the children:
1. Play in pairs, taking turns to throw the dice or spin a counter.
2. Move your counter forward the number thrown or spun. If you land on one of the 'collect card' spaces, take the appropriate picture card from the pile.
3. When you reach the 'Finish' square, go round again.
4. The winner is the first player to have all seven picture cards arranged in the correct order.

THE LIFE CYCLE

After the children have played the game, ask them to see whether they can arrange the life cycle cards in the correct order without referring to the gameboard.

ASSESSMENT
Note which children are able to perform the final task successfully.

IDEAS FOR DIFFERENTIATION
Children who have a confident grasp of the human life cycle could use the blank 'Wild cards' to add further stages to the game, either within childhood or within adult life. Children who are less sure about the human life cycle could be given sets of cards which are numbered consecutively. The stages of the life cycle could be reinforced with them through discussion after the game.

OTHER LIFE CYCLES

GROUP SIZE AND ORGANISATION
Groups of 4 to 6.
DURATION
15 minutes.
LEARNING OBJECTIVE
To compare the life cycles of other living creatures with that of the human, discovering more about similarities and differences between all living creatures.

YOU WILL NEED
Simple labelled diagrams showing the butterfly and frog life cycles (see Figures 5 and 6).

WHAT TO DO
Talk to the class about the life cycles of various animals. Using appropriate diagrams, talk them through the butterfly life cycle (see Figure 5): *butterfly... laying eggs... egg hatching into caterpillar, which eats leaves... caterpillar making a chrysalis... emerging as a new butterfly.* Discuss how this life cycle is different from ours, and highlight any similar principles. Do the same for the frog life cycle (see Figure 6): *frog... laying frog spawn in water... hatching as tadpoles... tadpole growing legs... climbing onto land as frog.*

Ask the children, working in groups, to think about the life cycle of a bird. Can they draw a diagram of the stages? They might come up with: *bird... egg... chick... bird.* It is important to keep the whole concept as simple as possible, in order for all of the children to reach the conclusion that all living things are part of a life cycle.

Ask the children to draw some life cycle diagrams for other creatures (perhaps using their experience of pets), and to place these alongside the human life cycle pictures they have made in earlier activities. Encourage them to identify similarities and differences.

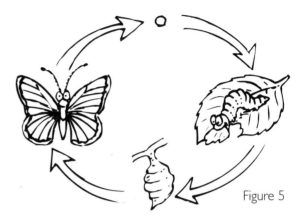

Figure 5

ASSESSMENT
Note (in discussion) which children show awareness that there are similarities and differences between humans and other living things.

IDEAS FOR DISPLAY
The children's drawings of various animal life cycles can be displayed alongside their pictures of the human life cycle in such a way as to invite comparisons. The children could produce further illustrations showing the butterfly and frog life cycles (see Figures 5 and 6).

IDEAS FOR DIFFERENTIATION
More confident children could research the theme of life cycles in general, looking at the different numbers of stages and the length of different animals' lives. *Which animals look after their children? Which do not? Why might this be?*

Less confident children could try to find out how many different life cycles can easily be broken down into three basic stages: egg, baby, adult. They could draw some of these life cycles and write labels.

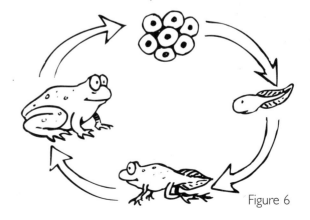

Figure 6

THE LIFE CYCLE

Name _____   Date _____

Stages of the human life cycle

Me as a baby aged _____	Me now aged _____
My parents aged _____	My grandparents aged _____

◆ Ask for some photos to put in these spaces.

The human life cycle game

The winner is the first player with a full set of seven cards.

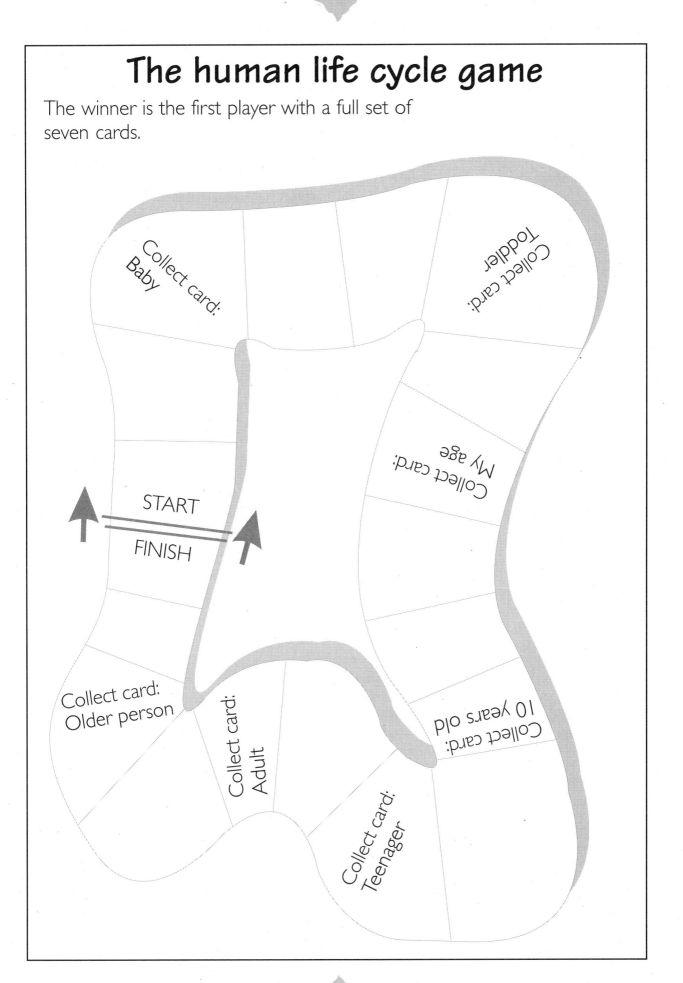

PHOTOCOPIABLE
RESOURCE
BANK

Human life cycle game cards